Wreathmaking
from the
State of Maine

Michele Maks

ISBN 089272-244-4
Library of Congress Catalog Card Number 87-72681

Design by Edith Allard
Printed at Alpine Press, Stoughton, Mass.

5   4   3   2   1

Down East Books
P.O. Box 679, Camden, Maine 04843

Wreathmaking
from the
State of Maine

Photographs by Joseph Dankowski

Sketches by Ellen Ketchum

Down East Books

Contents

Wreathmaking
from the
State of Maine

How I Became a Wreathmaker

The winter of 1982 was very wet. I wasn't selling my knitwear designs way back then; I was working in the woods with my husband, Jack. Or rather, I wasn't working in the woods with him—it was too wet. The tractor got stuck, and it was truly miserable.

Searching the want ads for something dry to do, I came across Ambrose McCarthy's advertisement for "Wreathmakers—will train." I had only made one wreath in my life, and it was a sickly looking thing, but anything seemed better than more rain down the back of my neck, so I called, set up an appointment with Barbara Kenney, and drove to Skowhegan.

At Ambrose's shop (which is also a bottle redemption center) I met Barbara, her daughter, and several other women who made wreaths from about the end of October to the first week or two of December every year. As I recall, there was only one wreathmaking machine there then. Some women worked in the shop, but many worked at home and brought in the finished wreaths.

There was a round of friendly banter going between Barbara and her daughter, who maintained that she could make wreaths better than Barbara because she'd had to learn by using the crummy brush that got dropped on the floor by the adults. (That's the way my fifteen-year-old learned, and it's true that she's a better wreathmaker than I am!)

Barbara showed me all the steps it took to make a good wreath. The first one I tried was lopsided, but it was definitely a wreath. The next one was good enough to sell. I don't mean to brag about catching on so quickly —on the contrary, it just proves how good a teacher Barbara is.

I made close to a hundred wreaths that first year, wholesaling most of them through McCarthy's, selling a few on the side over the phone mart, and giving them as gifts to all the New York relatives. Wreath making had saved the family finances and our tempers by providing reliable indoor work.

In following years we applied to craft fairs and sold wreaths at retail. Our booth is a wreathmaking "cave," of sorts, made out of poles lashed together. We decorate wreaths to order right on the spot, so there is always a crowd around the table choosing ribbons, waiting for wreaths, or asking questions. (One of the questions kids ask Jack is, "Are you Santa Claus?" He has white hair and a white beard.) Sometimes people would stop and examine our wreaths and say things like, "I didn't think they made them like this any more," or, "My mother used to make them when I was a kid, and they made the house smell so good." Others are interested in how our wreaths are constructed, having tried it themselves and ending up with a sickly looking wreath like my first attempt.

Making a wreath isn't hard, but there are a few things you have to know to get it right. That's why I wanted to write this book. Originally it was going to be entirely about evergreen wreaths. Until . . .

Having seen some beautiful dried flower wreaths at fairs, my daughter Quayl decided one summer to grow flowers to dry. She spent a great deal of time tending her flower beds. When it was time to harvest the flowers, we hung them to dry—and ended up with an awful mess! Many of the brilliant flowers completely faded, and all the statice dropped its petals. The entire harvest was lost. Putting in all that time and ending up with nothing to show for it prodded us to find out what had gone wrong, but there was very little information available that dealt with northern gardens or our specific problems.

Then I ran into Arthur Glickman at a United Maine Craftsmen Fair and asked if he would be interested in explaining a few things to me. He and his wife, Louise, through many years experience, have worked out the bugs (pardon the pun) of dried-flower raising in Maine. They knew immediately why our statice had dropped off! I was impressed, and I realized that maybe other would-be wreathmakers were looking for answers to the same problems.

The other types of wreaths in the book were included for similar reasons—as answers to questions people have asked me ("You're a wreathmaker? Maybe you can tell me why my grapevine wreath doesn't look good.") or as solutions to problems, like the cardboard boxes of seashells collected by the eleven kids who passed through here one summer (Throw them out? *Never!*).

Wreathmaking is a strictly seasonal occupation for my family. For me, it's a nice, if hectic, change of pace from designing sweaters. In fact, the wreathmaking was what made me go on to designing. I found that I really enjoyed the creating and marketing. Two of my books of sweater patterns will be published by New York City companies, and it's nice to be able to create, for one month of the year, something essentially Maine-ish.

Introduction

The word *wreath* comes from the Anglo-Saxon *wraeth*, which means "a twisted band." The earliest wreaths were found in the tombs of Egyptian pharaohs. They are a symbol of eternity, of everlasting life. Wreaths are used to crown conquerors, to embellish funeral processions, and to adorn brides on their wedding day. Today, in the United States, most people associate *wreath* with a circle of evergreen hung on a door during the Christmas season. A fragrant balsam wreath signals "welcome" to our circle of family and friends at Christmastime.

Barbara Kenney, of Skowhegan, started making wreaths at age twelve. Her grandmother and mother made them before her, beginning in the late 1930s. Wreathmaking, for Barbara, as it is now for many, was a family project. The menfolk worked in the woods cutting the large balsam trees for lumber and pulp. The women and children went out and cut the brush (balsam tips) in November for wreathmaking. The enterprising kids frequently chopped off the tops to peddle as Christmas trees. Barbara's daughter and daughter-in-law make wreaths now too, and Barbara expects that next year her thirteen-year-old grandson will be about ready to start.

Barbara's grandfather brought home discarded telephone wire to use for the hoop bases; wreath rings and rolls of wire weren't available back then. The bundles of brush were tied together separately with twine or yarn —whatever was around—and then tied on tightly on both sides of the homemade ring. Bows were cut from rolls of red crepe paper, and the wreath was finished off with a few pine cones. Then the children's arms were loaded up, and they sold the wreaths door to door. The retail price was fifteen cents apiece.

These days wreathmaking is big business in Maine. There are about a hundred wreath factories in the state producing three million wreaths for the Christmas sea-

Piles of wreaths at Central Maine Wreath Company.

Beginning a wreath on a wreathmaking machine.

son. The Maine Bureau of Agricultural Marketing publishes a brochure of mail-order wreath suppliers, and many catalogs sell Maine balsam wreaths. Fifty years ago, Barbara's grandmother made twenty-five or thirty wreaths per season at her kitchen table; today, Barbara's daughter can turn out a dozen good-looking wreaths on a wreath machine in twenty-five minutes.

Barbara has been a trainer and quality control supervisor at Central Maine Wreath, a Skowhegan wreath company, since it began in 1981. Ambrose McCarthy, the owner, says about two hundred local people are involved in the operation now. Some gather brush, some wind wreaths at home, some "pick" or "break" brush at the shop or work there winding wreaths by machine. Others make bows or decorate the finished wreaths.

In the Glickmans' garden.

Barbara is definitely picky about wreaths. McCarthy's wreaths weigh at least three pounds, and if you can see the joining place, well, you'd better take them somewhere else. A well-made wreath is truly an eternal circle with no beginning and no end.

Barbara's knowledge of wreathmaking was passed on to her by her mother and grandmother, but Arthur and Louise Glickman, of Clinton, learned most of what they know about dried flowers by trial and error. Since there is very little published information about everlastings, particularly for northern gardens, they learned a great deal by the painful process of making mistakes. From a small beginning (three plants) they have managed over the course of fifteen years to build a full-time business of selling dried flowers, arrangements, and floral and grapevine wreaths. They have also become walking encyclopedias on everlasting cultivation and harvesting.

In the Glickmans' workshop.

You don't have to live in Maine to make or enjoy these wreaths (although it helps!). Supply sources are listed at the end of the book for those who want to order materials or finished products. Visitors to Maine can take out the containers of seashells or pine cones the kids have hidden in the back of the closet, sit down in Ohio, Massachusetts, or Timbuktu, and make themselves a wreath from the glorious state of Maine.

Evergreen Wreaths

Gathering Brush

As with good soup, the secret to an attractive wreath is fresh ingredients. The more recently the brush has been cut, the longer the wreath will last. In order to avoid any legal trouble, check with the landowner before attempting to help yourself to greens on someone else's property. It's just courtesy to ask, and as common to obtain permission easily as it is to irritate someone by not asking. Of course, greens are available at many florists and craft stores and can be mail ordered.

Avoid diseased trees, which have telltale blisters and unusual yellow bumps on the needles. In general, it's better to cut brush from trees in low, wet areas, particularly if it has been a dry year. The needles will stay on the branches longer if the tree has been well watered all year long.

The most common and readily available types of evergreen in the Northeast are balsam, pine, hemlock, spruce, and cedar. Balsam is the most frequently used in commercial wreathmaking and is very long-keeping when cared for properly. Pine and cedar also keep fairly well. I recommend using spruce and hemlock only

[1.1] Clockwise from lower left: balsam, pine, hemlock, spruce, and cedar tips.

[1.2] Some balsam tips are fuller and more rounded than others. "Curly" brush is on left, flatter brush on right.

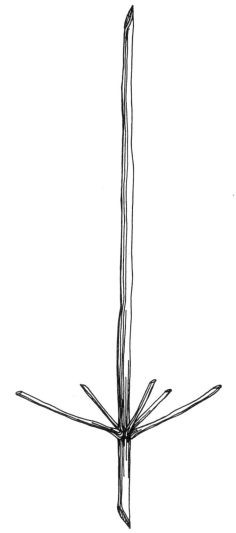

[Figure 1]

outdoors because, even when watered regularly, the needles dry out and drop off quickly once the tips are cut from the tree.

Balsam, the favorite, can look quite different depending on which part of the tree it comes from. "Curly" brush grows at the top of large trees, flatter brush at the bottom or on small trees. Very curly balsam looks much like spruce and makes the fullest, most appealing wreaths.

In commercial operations, the brush is gathered onto brush sticks (figure 1). These are merely small trees, de-limbed except for the bottom branches, which are stripped bare of brush. The bottom is chopped into a point for poking into the ground (or, more often, into the snow). Many pounds of brush can be slipped onto the pole in an overlapping circle, face down. A heavy string tied at the top and bottom makes an easy way to carry the brush stick once it is filled. The pole keeps the brush off the ground, and it can all be watered in one tidy place. If not used immediately, brush should be stored in a cool place, watered frequently, and *never* laid out on concrete. Contact with a garage or cellar floor rips up the needles and makes them unsightly and unusable.

Basic Balsam Wreath

The basic balsam wreath begins with a 12-inch-diameter wreath ring. The actual diameter of the finished wreath will be closer to 20 inches. A properly executed double-faced wreath will weigh a minimum of three pounds; if you are very generous with the brush, it may be five pounds or more.

The materials and tools you will need are:
   one 12-inch wreath ring
   a roll of heavy floral wire
   a pair of dykes (small brush clippers)

Basic balsam wreath decorated
with natural red berries and
clusters of spruce cones

[1.3]

[1.4]

[1.5]

boughs of fresh balsam
an extra pair of hands to help finish off your wreath
gloves, for those with sensitive hands
waterless hand-cleaner to remove pitch

Begin by "picking the brush"— clipping small pieces from the boughs (photo 1.3). Some people break the pieces with their hands, but I find it easier to clip them with the dykes. Several differently shaped pieces will be used to form bundles (photos 1.4 and 1.5). No cut edges are used except in the middle of a V-shaped piece, and then only if placed on the bottom of a bundle. For a nice-looking wreath, no cut edges must show.

The most important tip about making this type of wreath is to make your bundles uniform in size. There is no standard, only the size that fits your hand and feels comfortable. A practiced eye can tell if two wreaths

[1.6]

[1.7]

[1.8]

were made by different people—hand sizes vary. Sometimes it's helpful to make up a few bundles at a time.

Knot the wire onto the ring (photo 1.6) and wire on the first bundle (photo 1.7). Be sure to catch all ends. For beginners, wrapping the wire at least twice works best. When the first bundle is securely wired on, flip the entire ring over and wrap a second bundle on this side of the ring. Remember, this is a double-faced wreath, and you will be working back and forth on both sides of the ring. Continue to wire on bundles, one side to another, staggering the bundles slightly, with regular spaces in between bundles (photo 1.8). Work all the way around the ring until you are as close as you can get to the first two bundles.

It is probably wise to go find another pair of hands at this point, although it's certainly possible to finish off a wreath by yourself. You'll find that it is much easier to have someone hold back the ends of the first bundles

[1.9]

[1.10]

(photo 1.9), which have an annoying way of getting wrapped up with the last bundle's wiring. The intention is to push the cut edges of the last bundles as far as possible under the first one. Depending on how closely spaced your bundles are, it may be helpful to cut your last bundles shorter than all of the others. The wire should be wrapped around the last bundles several times, then snipped and poked down into the wreath.

The desired outcome is a wreath that has no beginning and no end (photo 1.10), or at least one that looks that way. If your finishing isn't perfect, don't despair; an uneven joining can be a great place to put your bow.

Now it's time to wash the pitch off your hands!

Variations on Basic Balsam Wreath

Hearts. A heart-shaped wreath can be made easily by bending a 12-inch ring into a heart shape (photo 1.11). The first two bundles should be a little longer than the rest. Begin at the bottom of the top V (photo 1.12). These pieces will hang down into the center and also cover the cut edges of the last bundles. Continue wrapping bundles around as for the basic balsam wreath until you arrive back at the other side of the top V. Finish the wreath by securing the cut edges of the last two bundles underneath the overhanging first bundles (photo 1.13). As with the round wreaths, it is advisable to cut the last two bundles a little shorter than

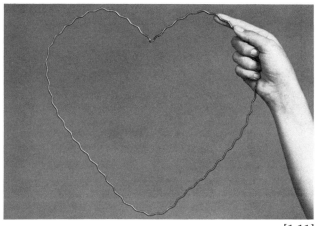

[1.11]

[1.12]

[1.13]

all the rest. Hearts are easier to finish because it isn't necessary to achieve a perfect circle, and the first bundles do a good job of hiding the last cut edges.

Larger Wreaths. The rule is: the bigger the wreath, the bigger and longer the brush. On a 20-inch diameter wreath ring, the length of the bundles might be about 8 to 10 inches. It is very useful to have big hands for this large a wreath. The construction is the same as for a 12-inch wreath, with more muscle power needed to turn the ring over each time.

Smaller Wreaths. The smallest commercial wreath ring I've ever found is eight inches, so for our smallest wreaths — 5-inch ring diameter — we create our own rings. An ordinary coat hanger is straightened and the wire wrapped once around a 5-inch base (a juice can works fine) and the ends are welded together. It also works to twist the ends of the wire together if a welder is not available.

A 20-inch balsam wreath decorated with white-pine cones

Heart made of balsam and cedar

A 5-inch hemlock wreath

A 12-inch spruce and pine wreath

These wreaths are a good way to use up brush that is too short to use on a 12-inch ring. Small brush *must* be used or there will be no "center" to the wreath. Construction is the same as for a 12-inch wreath, with small hands having a definite advantage in this case.

Hemlock is very effective in this size wreath because the needles are so small, but it should only be used outdoors. A wreath this size made of balsam makes a cute indoor decoration. If fresh brush is used and the wreath is misted with water from a plant mister every few days, the balsam wreath can be kept indoors safely for the entire holiday season.

Other Types of Brush

Cedar has very lacelike foliage, and when used on the underside it adds a lighter green color to a wreath. It works very well with balsam for the heart-shaped wreaths, adding a feminine touch all its own. I don't recommend using it alone; it takes enormous quantities to fill out a whole wreath, and the needles appear droopy without any firmer brush to hold them up. Also, the smell of just plain cedar isn't as nice as balsam.

Pine also works best as an accent because of its long needles. Mixed with spruce or balsam, it makes an elegant country-style wreath. It is sometimes difficult to find pine without a lot of yellow needles, but these can be pulled out easily.

Spruce makes the crispest-looking wreaths, but it has two serious drawbacks: it doesn't keep well once cut and therefore should be used only outdoors, and it has very sharp needles. Bluntly put (no pun intended), working with spruce can be extremely painful. It does make a very attractive wreath, so the discomfort might be worth it to some. Gloves help, but I don't recommend making many spruce wreaths in one season.

Hemlock is as soft as spruce is sharp. Because it tends to droop, it is effective alone only on small wreaths.

Again, because it dries out quickly, it should be used outdoors only.

Princess Pine is an evergreen plant that retains its color long after picking, but I would urge people *not* to pick it. There are very few places where it remains growing naturally. While not actually on an endangered species list, it is rare enough that picking should be discouraged. If for some reason you must harvest it, cutting pieces selectively with shears is the least destructive method; pulling the plant up by the roots will destroy it.

Again, I want to emphasize: do not harvest any greens on someone else's land without first obtaining permission. Taking plants or brush from another's property without express permission is *stealing*.

Care of Brush Wreaths

Like freshly gathered brush, finished wreaths should never be laid down on a cement floor, because cement tears up the needles. Piling wreaths has a tendency to flatten them. We (my family) keep large quantities of wreaths hanging on long poles in an outdoor shed. We turn them every day and spray them with water every few days.

A wreath hung on an outside door should not need any care in northern climates if it is made of fresh balsam brush. In warmer climates, or if the wreath is made of spruce or hemlock, spraying with water from a plant mister is recommended. Any wreath kept indoors should be misted every few days. In these days when many people choose to have an artificial Christmas tree, an indoor balsam wreath, properly cared for, can impart that special Christmasy atmosphere.

Cone Wreaths

Cone wreaths have an advantage over evergreen ones in that they can be used for more than one season. Handled with care, a cone wreath should last for many years. The oldest pinecone wreath I know of has been around about fifteen years. The owner sprays it a different color every year and trims it with a matching bow. When the holiday season approaches, her neighbors begin to ask, "What color'll it be this year?" One year it was pink, another year baby blue. She says, "I like to be untraditional."

[2.1] Clockwise from upper left: white-pine cone, red-pine cone, acorn, spruce cone, hemlock cone.

The most common cones in Maine are pine (white, red, or Norway), spruce, and hemlock. Similar long-lived wreaths are made from the plentiful acorns. But-

ternuts and beechnuts are also found in southern Maine, but are not common. Cone and nut gatherers, like brush gatherers, should respect landowners' property rights. Many people who have large evergreen trees in their yards are delighted when someone wants to pick up "all those darn cones." If no natural sources are available, craft and hobby stores usually carry a good selection of cones and nuts at Christmastime.

Cone wreaths can be made in several different ways. Three of them are described here.

Entirely Wired Cone Wreath

For this wreath you will need:
    a cone wreath ring
    heavy floral wire
    dykes (small brush clippers)
    needle-nosed pliers
    an assortment of white-pine cones
    an assortment of nuts with holes drilled in them so
        they can be wired
    waterless hand-cleaner to remove pitch

The cones should be dampened with a mister several hours before working with them. This will close their "petals" so the cones can be packed more tightly onto the ring.

Drilling the nuts takes some care and patience. We use a very old Drexel hobby grinder/polisher, without the head attached, because it makes a very lightweight, safe tool for drilling the nuts. (So simple that the kids can do it.) Using this tool, the nuts can be safely held in the hand while drilling. A larger drill can be used instead, but it requires more care, and the nuts have to be held in a vise. Use a fine bit—$1/16$ inch or less.

The "hill" part of the ring is the front side. Twist lengths of wire around the individual pine cones (about in the center, and pushed down between the "petals") and wire a row of cones crosswise around the

Entirely wired cone wreath made
with white pine cones and acorns

[2.2]

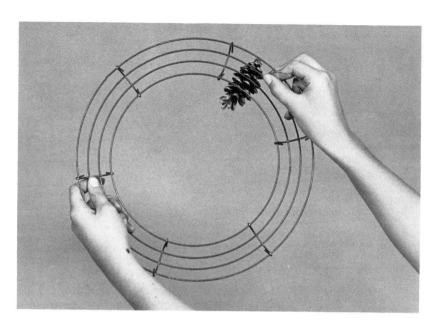

front side of the ring, forming a center row (photo 2.3). Then wire cones on the innermost and outermost edges of the ring in the opposite direction, fitting them in as tightly as possible. When the entire ring is covered with white-pine cones, run wire through the drilled nuts and acorns and wire them into the ring in any remaining spaces.

Working on the back side, twist all wires tightly with the needle-nosed pliers. Cut all wires closely with the dykes and fold the pokey wire ends toward the front side of the wreath. When the cones dry, they will open up once again and more completely fill the spaces.

This wreath is left natural and unsprayed. If left outdoors, it will weather much as barn boards do. A wire loop can be tied on for a hanger, or the wreath can be hung on a nail on its own frame.

Wired and Glued Cone Wreath

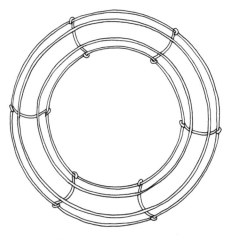

[Figure 2]

For this wreath you will need:
  a cone wreath ring (figure 2)
  heavy floral wire
  dykes (small brush clippers)
  needle-nosed pliers with wire cutter
  an assortment of white- and red-pine cones
  an assortment of smaller nuts and cones (butternuts,
       acorns, and spruce cones are shown)
  hot glue melted in a double boiler, or a hot-glue gun
  a spray can of clear lacquer
  waterless hand-cleaner to remove pitch

All cones should be dampened with a mister several hours before working with them so cones will close up and be easier to pack closely together. The "hill" part of the ring is the front side.

With the front side facing, work white-pine cones over the first outside wire, force them under the next inner wire (figure 3), and wire them on in this position. Do this all the way around in a loose starburst formation. Then work more white-pine cones over the first inside wire and under the next inner wire in a smaller but similar pattern. Next, wire red-pine cones, either right-side up or upside down, all the way around the ring between the two rows of white-pine cones, covering their inside edges.

The rest is done with hot glue. Use liberal quantities to attach the smaller butternuts, acorns, and spruce cones in an attractive "filling-in" pattern. Placement is left entirely to individual taste and the amount of space there is to fill. When all spaces are covered, let the wreath dry thoroughly.

When the cones have opened up and are completely dry, spray several light coats of clear lacquer on the wreath and allow it to dry again.

A wire loop can be tied on for a hanger, or the wreath can be hung on a nail on its own frame.

[Figure 3]

Wired and glued cone wreath made
with a variety of cones and nuts

Entirely glued cone wreath made
with spruce cones

Entirely Glued Cone Wreath

For this wreath you will need:
    a circle of cardboard, light plywood, or masonite for a
        wreath base
    hot glue or strong craft cement
    a collection of small, light cones (only spruce cones
        are used in the wreath shown, but hemlock
        cones can be added)
    a bow, if desired
    a spray can of clear lacquer

This is probably the simplest of the cone wreaths, and it makes a good children's project with some supervision. Small cones, such as spruce and hemlock, are *not* misted before using.

Cut the base material to the desired size and shape. (It is by no means necessary to stick to a standard wreath circle.) Dip the cones in hot glue, or apply cement liberally, and set them on the base. A starburst pattern is the most conducive to filling up space, but any placement that covers the surface and is pleasing is acceptable. Holes can always be filled in with smaller hemlock cones—or holly berries, for a touch of color (real holly sprigs are nicest, of course, but the plastic berries will last longer).

When all cones are applied, let the glued wreath dry completely. Spray with several light coats of clear lacquer and let the wreath dry again. A bow can be glued on or wired through a hole poked in the base. A picture hanger can be glued to the back of the base for hanging, or a hole can be made in the base for hanging on a nail.

Other Types of Wreaths

Grapevine Wreath

For this wreath you will need:
   grapevines, wild or domestic
   pruning shears
   heavy floral wire
   5-gallon plastic bucket or other round base

The best time to harvest grapevines is in late winter or early spring. If you have domesticated grapes, the prunings make excellent wreaths. The vines at this stage (early spring) are juicy and pliable. If you are working with wild grapevines, cut only the thinnest of last year's growth. A good healthy grapevine should produce eight to ten feet of new growth in a season. This is long enough for a wreath.

If the only time you can harvest vines is in the summer or fall (and this is when they are most recognizable, as there are leaves and grapes on them!), soak the vines for several days to a week before using. This will make them more bendable. Avoid thick, woody vines; even with soaking, they are hard to work with and are unattractive at the cut edge.

Cut the vines with pruning shears. If there are leaves, remove them, but be careful to keep tendrils intact. These curly twists are one of the charming characteristics of a grapevine wreath and should be left on whenever possible.

A "jig," or base, makes the wreath winding easier. The bottom of a 5-gallon plastic bucket works well and is a good size for a wreath. Wrap the first vines around and around the sides of the bucket and fasten them together with floral wire. After winding around the bucket a couple of times, remove this circle of vines

Grapevine wreath

and begin to wind more vine around it, weaving in and around the original circle. Keep adding vines, attaching them with floral wire if necessary, circling around and in and out. There is no set number of times to go around—whatever looks good is right. Shorter vines can be woven between the longer vines to fill out a wreath if few long vines are available.

The finished wreath should be left to dry for a week or two in a warm, well-ventilated place. When vines are completely dried out, the floral wire may be removed—the dried wreath will keep its shape.

Beginners should be advised that one becomes more dexterous with grapevines with practice, and the more wreaths you do, the better they will look.

[3.1] Grapevines harvested in summer must be trimmed and soaked before using.

Stick Wreath

My interest in stick wreaths was inspired by the clumps of red osier dogwood growing at the edge of our woods. The smooth, glossy stalks have a bright red color that is very suitable for a holiday wreath.

For this wreath you will need:
  plywood, hammer, nails, and compass (to construct frame)
  heavy floral wire
  needle-nosed pliers
  a bundle of pliable sticks (at least 12 inches long)

Stick wreaths are similar to grapevine wreaths. They can be made of nearly any thin, pliable sticks. New tree growth in fields can be used if it's not too thick and woody. All sticks need to be soaked several days to be workable.

Because sticks are shorter and stiffer than vines, a frame is needed to mold them. This can be made easily out of a piece of plywood with nails pounded in at intervals to form both an inside and outside circle (figure 4). Lay strips of wire on the frame first, radiating outward between the nails, then lay sticks between the concentric circles of nails, filling in the entire circumference. When the desired fullness is achieved, wrap the strips of wire around the sticks and tighten them with pliers.

[Figure 4]

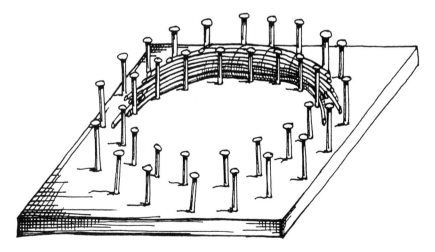

Stick wreath made from red osier
dogwood

The wreath should stay in the frame until completely dry. Unlike grapevine wreaths, which "set" into their final shape as they dry, stick wreaths need the wires to hold them together even after drying.

Wrapping the wreath with coordinating ribbon is an attractive way to decorate it.

Seashell Wreath

Anyone who visits the seashore with children will come home with a pailful (at least!) of souvenirs from the trip. Kids are delighted by any kind of shell, and even the most insignificant broken shell can become a treasure to its finder. A seashell wreath is a less traditional, less seasonal sort of decoration, and it is one that can be made by a child with some adult supervision.

You will need:
   cardboard
   compass
   mat knife or heavy scissors for cutting cardboard
   craft cement or melted hot glue
   a spray can of clear lacquer
   a collection of Maine coast seashells

Examine all shells carefully for "residents." Any still containing live creatures, or parts of them, should be discarded quickly before they become a smelly nuisance. Wash the rest in hot, soapy water, using a scrub brush if necessary. Dry the shells thoroughly before beginning to glue them onto the wreath. This process can be speeded up by putting the shells in a slow oven until dry, but don't turn the heat up too high or leave them in too long or they will become too brittle to use.

Cut a circle out of cardboard, using a compass to mark the desired size. Beginning with the largest shells of the collection, glue them securely on the cardboard, using liberal quantities of glue or cement and covering the surfaces as completely as possible. A starburst shape is probably the most conducive to covering large areas,

Seashell wreath made pri-
marily of mussel shells

but any pattern will do. When the surface is covered as much as possible with larger shells, use smaller ones to fill in the spaces.

I use the word *shells* here very loosely. Children take a particular interest in bits of smooth glass, crab carapaces, and weathered pieces of driftwood, and any such "treasures" certainly can be used.

When all shells are set in place, leave the wreath undisturbed until the glue or cement is completely dry and set.

When it's dry, spray the wreath with several light coats of clear lacquer and then allow it to dry again. A picture hanger can be glued to the back of the cardboard, or a small hole can be poked in the cardboard to hang it on a nail.

The finished wreath can be displayed year-round, a cheerful reminder of a pleasant day at the beach.

[Figure 5]

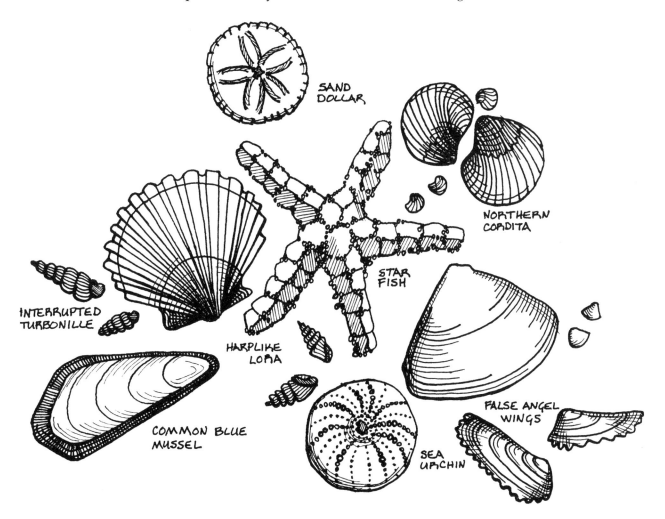

Dried Flower Wreaths

Growing Your Own Everlastings

This is not intended to be a handbook on raising flowers for drying, but I can point out certain problems that beginners dabbling with growing everlastings consistently encounter. Arthur and Louise Glickman, who have been growing and drying many different types of flowers in Clinton, Maine, for the last fifteen years, have this advice for beginners.

Not all flowers can be dried successfully. Many beautiful blooms in the garden are total failures as dried flowers. Your best bet is to look in the "everlastings" section of your usual seed catalog or to check with an experienced drier in your area.

It is very tempting for a beginner to order packets of mixed colors. This can be disappointing because some colors are hardier and germinate faster than others. If a mixed packet is started early indoors and only the largest, hardiest seedlings are saved, most of the different colors are going to be discarded. If all colors are desired, it is much better to buy a packet of each color and to treat them as separate plants.

Color names can be confusing, and this is made worse by their variation from catalog to catalog and from year to year. There are six basic colors: white, yellow, red, pink, purple, and bronze/copper. There are varying tones among these colors, but if a seed catalog reads "rouge," "scarlet," or "dark rose," you can guess that what you'll be getting is some tone of red. Most names suggesting blue are actually going to give you a variation of purple. Blue is the most difficult true color to obtain in the flower world.

Following is a basic list of everlastings that are quite popular for home-dried flowers.

Statice, which comes in many colors, is a staple for wreaths. It does best in a well-drained soil. The most common problem is botrytis, an invisible fungus triggered by damp, cool weather. It frequently hits only late fall crops. This is a particularly destructive fungus, as it makes the flower heads fall off the dried flowers. Anyone growing statice should test for the fungus in the garden by gently running a hand from stalk to flower tops; if the flowers fall off with just this light contact, botrytis is there. It attacks in blocks of color, with white and yellow flowers being hit first. Treatment with a commercial fungicide can save the crop.

Statice is ready to dry when the bottom flowers on the stalk begin to open. Hang the stalks upside down in a well-ventilated place to dry. When the stalks are stiff, store them in covered bags to prevent fading.

Strawflowers are particularly easy to grow. In a well-fertilized garden, the standard varieties can grow tall enough to blow down and break off, but the plant will usually grow back from the base.

A common problem is a very visible cottony growth on the stalks, called white mold. This can kill the whole plant and is made worse by wet soil. It is treated by a fungicide.

Strawflowers are harvested when the second layer of petals on the bottom begins to open. It's important to pick on a sunny afternoon because the petals close up more in the evening and early morning or on overcast days. Pick strawflowers early. If the center petals have begun to open, the flowers will be too far gone to dry well.

Flowers are picked off and laid on newspapers or stuck on the end of 12-inch pieces of floral wire to dry (French 22-gauge green wire is recommended). The flower heads will dry onto the wire and stay attached. This way they can be used in arrangements.

Lunaria is also called money plant, silver shillings, or poor man's dollars. Most people don't realize that it is a biennial and takes two years to mature. The first spring it forms a taproot; the next spring it flowers, and in mid-August forms its distinctive silver coins. Because it has a taproot, it does best in well-drained soil and does not do well in cool, wet years.

The whole plant is harvested in the fall. It is fairly sturdy with the shells left on the coins and should be stored this way. When you're ready to use it, peel off the outer shells to reveal the silvery color of the dollars. They are very delicate in the uncovered state and will tear quite easily.

Silvery Gray Artemesia is a practically indestructible perennial. Plant it where it can take over, because it spreads rapidly. It should be harvested late in the summer when pinhead-sized flowers appear at the top. Hang upside down in bunches to dry. It can be used almost immediately.

Pearly Everlasting Celosia (crested type) is a northern roadside plant that is easily transferred to the home garden. The heads are made up of groups of small white flowers. It should be harvested as soon as the white flowery parts appear—it is too late when the yellow stamens are showing. Hang upside down to dry.

Yellow Yarrow has a eucalyptus-type smell, and it's large, flat head consists of hundreds of flowerets. It is better to buy plants than seeds to grow this plant. Yarrow is very susceptible to the tarnished plant bug, a quarter-inch-long brownish or greenish insect that can do a lot of damage in a flower garden. The insect's saliva poisons the plants, and the flowers become discolored and misshapen. Yellow yarrow is useful as a "red flag" for this pest in a flower garden; the bug is more visible on the yarrow and its appearance there can be a signal to treat other plants. A mild insecticide will control it.

Yellow yarrow should be harvested when fully open and hung upside down in bunches to dry. It can be used almost immediately.

Hardy German Statice is a branchy perennial with large, flat flower heads. It is all white, with very small flowers. Pick it when two thirds of the flowers are open, and hang the plants upside down by the stems until stiff. The heads are broken up in pieces to use on wreaths.

Baby's Breath has a tiny seed, so it is better to grow it from plants rather than from seed. It is the *perennial* type that is used for dried flowers. The plant's heavy taproot will rot in wet soil, so plant it in a well-drained location.

Pick the plants when the flowers are just beginning to open, and hang them upside down to dry. The baby's breath sold in florist and craft stores is quite often flocked (sprayed with a cottony material) and dyed. In its natural state, it is white and very delicate.

Accrolinum is a pink or white daisylike flower with a yellow center. It is a prolific annual, sometimes susceptible to aphids. Pick these flowers, on the stem, as soon as they begin to open and hang them upside down to dry. One drawback of accrolinum is that the flowers are very delicate and difficult to store.

Globe Amaranth. The flowers of this slow-growing plant resemble clover blooms (which do not work as dried flowers). The white, purple, or orange heads are pickable when they measure about one half to three quarters of an inch in diameter. (They shred when dry if they are over one inch across.) Pick the heads off the stems and lay them out on newspapers to dry. The smaller heads are tough and store well; the larger they are, the more carefully they need to be handled.

Grains such as wheat, barley, and rye, are all fairly easy to grow in small quantities. The older varieties seem to produce the most decorative awns. Pick the stalks before you would harvest them for grain—when the kernels are creamy, not milky. (Admittedly, this is a subtle distinction. The best description I can offer is this: If the kernels are pressed with a thumbnail and a watery juice squirts out, they are not mature enough, but neither should the kernels be entirely dry.) If harvested too late, the heads will shatter.

All the flowers listed above, if planted in the north, should be started indoors about the same time you'd start tomatoes. Seedlings are often available at florists or greenhouses; if not, most greenhouses will take special orders for particular plants.

Dried flower wreath of statice,
lunaria, and strawflowers

Any plant production depends on soil fertility. Poor soil will produce unhealthy, low-yielding plants. Garden sanitation is a good preventative to many insect and disease problems, and black plastic mulch can help keep down weeds.

Although silica gel is often recommended for speeding up the drying process, the Glickmans advise against it. Silica frequently dries flowers so quickly that it blackens them. The dust has been known to cause silicosis, a serious lung condition, so always wear a mask while working with it. All of the natural drying techniques described above are safe, although not speedy, and they do require that you pay close attention to your garden to catch flowers at their optimum drying times. Masses of drying flowers make a fragrant and decorative addition to any home or workshop, so the extra drying time required by the natural drying method need not be a hardship.

Dried Flower Wreath

You will need:
  a straw wreath base
  a hot-glue gun
  floral hot-glue sticks (clear)
  an assortment of dried flowers

The easiest and most common type of dried flower wreath begins with a commercial straw wreath base. These are available at almost any florist or craft supply store. Although many ways of attaching the flowers are possible (pins, wire, sticking stems into the base), the most long-lasting is to use hot glue. A hot-glue gun (photo 4.1) seems to work better in this case than just dipping the flowers in melted glue.

Stems should be broken off short enough that the flowers can be placed easily on the wreath. Apply glue to the stems and place them on the straw base in an overlapping pattern (photo 4.2). Continue around the straw base, taking care to arrange flowers in a pleasing

[4.1]

[4.2]

[4.3]

[4.4]

pattern of color and texture (photo 4.3). Flowers with just heads are glued on to cover the stems. The finished color pattern should be pleasing to the eye should not be absolutely symmetrical (photo 4.4).

Dried-flower wreaths should be hung away from direct sunlight, which will fade the flowers.

Decorations

Wreath decorations are strictly a matter of taste. For every person who thinks it's traditional to place the bow at the top, there's one who thinks it's traditional to hang the bow at the bottom. At fairs I decorate wreaths to order, most of the time with a crowd of people waiting and watching. Everyone wants to know how to tie a bow. The first year, out of desperation, I invented my own foolproof (and I might add hassleproof) method of making a bow. With very little practice, one can make this bow in public while discoursing on politics, the weather, and the low price of someone else's wreaths. In a pinch, I can make one in my sleep.

You'll need:
  A roll of ribbon, any width
  a 10-inch to 16-inch-long piece of floral wire, depend
      ing on width of ribbon and size of bow
  scissors

The secret to this bow is that it is folded, not tied. The ribbon is left attached to the roll until the bow is nearly finished. Pull ribbon from the roll until you have the length desired for the first tail. Holding it at this point, pull more ribbon until you have a loop. Twist wire around the loop at this point (photo 5.1). Pull up another loop, a little smaller than the first, and twist that loop with the wire (photo 5.2). If you are working with very narrow ribbon, or if you want to make a large fluffy bow, continue making these loops on this side until you have three, four, or even five loops. Now make the same number of loops on the other side of the bow (photo 5.3), twisting wire around each loop and taking care to make this second set of loops approximately the same size as the first set. Pull the roll of ribbon down to the end of the first tail, and cut the second tail the same length. Take care that the tails are symmetrical on both sides of the bow.

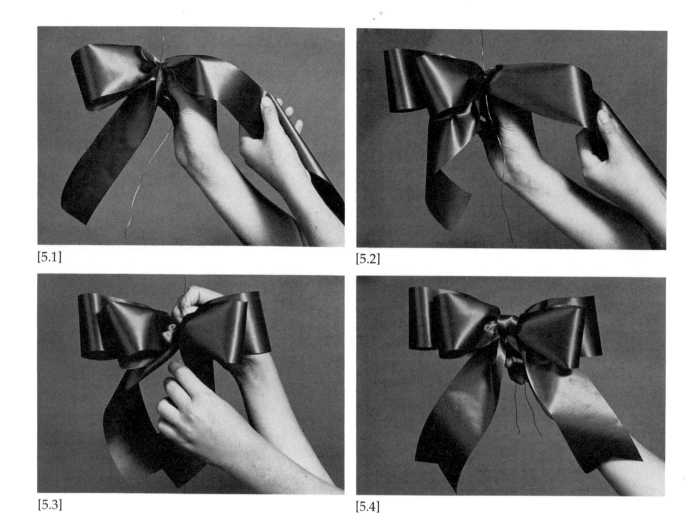

[5.1]

[5.2]

[5.3]

[5.4]

Cut a center for the bow by snipping a two- to three-inch piece of ribbon from the roll. This center is wrapped between the two sets of loops and tails and twisted in back of the bow with the ends of the wire (photo 5.4). The cut ends of this "center" will stick out at the back of the bow and can be stuck between pieces of brush on your wreath to stabilize the bow. The tail ends of the ribbon are snipped either diagonally or in a W-shape to prevent fraying.

Cones and nuts make the easiest, most inexpensive decorations. They can be used singly or in clusters. Of course, all sorts of plastic, wooden, and tinsel decorations are available commercially, but we much prefer the natural Maine products. Seashells can be wired onto an evergreen wreath to good effect.

Wrapping stick, grapevine, and cone wreaths with ribbon is very popular and easy to do. Simply wind it around and around the wreath, taking care to pull the ribbon snugly. Fasten the ends together with pins or wire.

My kids like our wreath decorated with a teddy-bear-print bow and one of their dressed-up teddies sitting in the center.

Supply Sources from the State of Maine

A mail-order catalog of wreaths, craft books, and hand-loomed knitwear is available from Michele Maks at:

Dear Run Farm
RFD #4, Box 5535
Farmington, ME 04938

Wreathmaking Supplies

Kelco Industries
Milbridge, Maine 04658
207-546-7541 (or 800-343-4057, out of state)

Wreaths

Freshly made balsam wreaths both retail and wholesale, are available at the shop and through the mail from Ambrose McCarthy. (Native Maine maple syrup, blue-berry jam, and honey are also available with or without wreaths.) Large wholesale quantities are available for fundraising groups throughout the United States. Contact:

Central Maine Wreath Company
330 North Avenue
Skowhegan, Maine 04976
207-474-8837

A brochure on mail-order sources of Maine wreaths, Christmas trees, and other agricultural products is available from:

Maine Dept. of Agriculture, Food,
   and Rural Resources
Station 28
Augusta, Maine 04333
207-289-3491

Dried Flower Wreaths and Supplies

The Glickmans grow and sell air-dried strawflowers and statice in a wide range of natural colors for wreath-making and arrangements. They also offer ten to fifteen other species of dried flowers that fill out and add texture to a wreath. Grapevine and straw bases are also available from them.

Fourteen-inch wreaths are available by mail order. No two are alike, and they can be ordered in a dominant tone or color, covered with brilliant flowers grown in Maine. The 1987 price is $18.50, postage paid. For more information contact:

Arthur and Louise Glickman
RFD 2
Clinton, ME 04927
207-426-2744
(Please include a SASE)

For those interested in growing their own flowers for drying, here are recommended seed suppliers. For varieties proven successful in northern gardens, contact:

Johnny's Selected Seeds
Albion, ME 04910
207-437-9294

Other recommended suppliers, out-of-state:
Park Seed Company
Cokesbury Road
Greenwood, SC 29647-0001
1-803-223-7333

Stokes Seeds Inc.
737 Main St., Box 548
Buffalo, NY 14240
1-716-672-8844

Acknowledgments

This book would not have been written without the help of many people. Thank you to Barbara Kenney, for sharing so generously her family history and techniques for winding evergreen wreaths; Ambrose McCarthy, for opening up Central Maine Wreath for a photo session; Arthur and Louise Glickman for explaining so painstakingly their art and craft and for becoming good friends in the process; friends Joe D. and Ellen for the wonderful photos and sketches; Polly Carson and Quayl Rewinski, the "hands" in the wreath construction photos; Bill and Emily Hastings, Peggy Titcomb, and Jeanne Sawyer of the Farmington Public Library for use of their decorative front doors; Tobin, Tobias, and Polly Carson, and Quayle Rewinski for appearing as "the kids" in this book; and last but not least, thanks to Jack, who put up with it all and, as usual, supported me two hundred percent.

Michele Maks exercises her creative talents as a wreath-maker and a designer of knitted and crocheted items. She is also active in Upcountry Artists, a group formed to promote visual and performing arts. Her family's 165-acre farm is in Farmington, Maine.

Artist **Ellen Ketchum**, also from Farmington, Maine, has done illustrations for Maine Organic Farmers and Gardeners Association publications and also gives basketry workshops around the state.

Photographer **Joseph Dankowski** lives in Shirley Mills, Maine. His work has been seen in many shows and is included in the collection of New York's Museum of Modern Art.